ANTI IN
DIET

ACTION PLAN: 6 WEEK MEAL PLANS TO HEAL YOURSELF WITH FOOD, RESTORE OVERALL HEALTH AND BECOME PAIN FREE

© Copyright 2015 by Matheus Sartor & Jonathan Brum - All rights reserved.

This document is geared towards providing exact and reliable information in regards to the topic and issue covered. The publication is sold with the idea that the publisher is not required to render accounting, officially permitted, or otherwise, qualified services. If advice is necessary, legal or professional, a practiced individual in the profession should be ordered.

- From a Declaration of Principles which was accepted and approved equally by a Committee of the American Bar Association and a Committee of Publishers and Associations.

In no way is it legal to reproduce, duplicate, or transmit any part of this document in either electronic means or in printed format. Recording of this publication is strictly prohibited and any storage of this document is not allowed unless with written permission from the publisher. All rights reserved.

The information provided herein is stated to be truthful and consistent, in that any liability, in terms of inattention or otherwise, by any usage or abuse of any policies, processes, or directions contained within is the solitary and utter responsibility of the recipient reader. Under no circumstances will any legal responsibility or blame be held against the publisher for any reparation, damages, or monetary loss due to the information herein, either directly or indirectly.

Respective authors own all copyrights not held by the publisher.

The information herein is offered for informational purposes solely, and is universal as so. The presentation of the information is without contract or any type of guarantee assurance.

The trademarks that are used are without any consent, and the publication of the trademark is without permission or backing by the trademark owner. All trademarks and brands within this book are for clarifying purposes only and are the owned by the owners themselves, not affiliated with this document.

TABLE OF CONTENTS

Introduction 7

Chapter 1 - Inflammation – An Overview and A Comment 8

Chapter 2 - Foods that Aggravate Inflammation 11

    Specific Foods to Avoid... 12

Chapter 3 - Anti-Inflammatory Foods 13

    Avocado 13

    Ginger 13

    Turmeric 14

    Garlic 14

    Beetroot 14

    Asparagus 15

    Flax Seeds 15

    Cinnamon 15

    Green Tea 16

    Organic Red Wine 16

    Dark Chocolate 16

Chapter 4 - Six Week Action Plan 17

Step 1 – Restock Kitchen and Go Grocery Shopping........... 17

Step 2 – Print Out Both Meal Plan as well as Daily Schedule 18

Step 3 – Sample Meal Plan for a Week............... 20

Chapter 5 - Anti-Inflammatory Recipes 25

Breakfast Foods 25

   Cherry Coconut Porridge.................25

   Raspberry and Avocado Smoothie 27

   Gingerbread Oatmeal 28

   Chia Pudding 30

Lunch Foods 31

   Mediterranean Tuna Salad...............31

   Kale Caesar Salad with Grilled Chicken Wrap...............33

   Winter Fruit Salad 35

   Roasted Red Pepper and Sweet Potato Soup..................37

   Whole Wheat Pasta with Super Kale, Hemp and Flaxseed Oil Pesto............ 39

Dinner Foods 41

   Curried Potatoes with Poached Eggs 41

Baked Tilapia with Pecan Rosemary Topping 43

Italian-Style Stuffed Red Peppers 45

Snacks 47

Whole Wheat Tortilla and Hummus 47

Kale, Banana and Almond Milk Smoothie 48

Dark Chocolate and Nut Clusters 49

Spicy Watermelon and Pistachios 50

Chapter 6 - Things to Remember During your Six Week Action Plan 51

Establish a Support System before you Begin 51

Experiment with the Recipes 52

Maintain a Food Journal 52

Conclusion 53

Check Out My Other Books 57

INTRODUCTION

Inflammation is one of the main contributors to a number of diseases, from arthritis to Parkinson's disease, to even cancer! A lot of people suffer from chronic inflammation, but very few are able to identify and take the steps required to keep it under control.

One of the best ways to keep chronic inflammation under wraps is by making changes to your diet and your overall lifestyle. When we say the word 'diet', people tend to automatically assume that it is only for weight loss. Add to this the fact that a diet is a rather transitory ideology and most people are disappointed that they don't see results within the meal-plans they try out. Ideally, instead of trying out a diet for just a few weeks, you'll need to switch it up completely and make yourself a *lifestyle* change – the diet plans you follow should be a precursor to it, since going back to your previous diet regimen after you finish your meal-plan is only going to bring it all back!

In this book, we will take a look at some meal plans that you can follow to heal yourself with food! We will take a look at why these plans work, how they boost your immune system and prevent inflammation and check out recipes that you can make on your own! Remember – following an action plan is only to get you kick-started. Once the six-week trial ends, you will have to continue on this path to maintain the lifestyle, otherwise your inflammation is going to make a comeback!

Thanks again for purchasing this book. I hope you enjoy it!

CHAPTER 1

INFLAMMATION – AN OVERVIEW AND A COMMENT

Inflammation, as a process, can be both acute and chronic. It is the body's way of protecting itself from injury or infections. When you observe it from the outside, inflammation is easily identified through its symptoms such as heat and swelling of the tissue, pain in the affected area, fluid accumulation, redness, etc.

What is essentially happening is that your immune system is responding to foreign bodies to protect you; however, in diseases like rheumatoid arthritis, the body isn't attacking any foreign object, but your own tissues – the immune system has gone wonky and is making antibodies to hurt your own body. This is known as an autoimmune disorder.

Now, in simple terms, to make sure inflammation doesn't keep you from leading a healthy and happy life, we are going to focus on how you can modify your daily food patterns and change your lifestyle to help you handle your inflammation. The foods we eat have to boost our immune system instead of causing it to act out – you need to not only try an action meal plan for a few weeks, but make it part of your daily lifestyle so that it sticks and inflammation doesn't make a comeback!

The problem with most people is that they tend to assume that these kinds of diets, whether for weight loss or inflammation, are *curative* – they are not. Sustained weight loss or keeping your chronic inflammation under control is not something that can magically happen overnight; these require lifestyle changes with certain staples, such as regular exercise, healthy eating, proper sleep, etc., becoming an instinct. You cannot finish a 6-week action plan and then go back to your previous life – that will simply undo whatever you've worked so hard for and bring all the negatives back.

So, essentially, what you should do is to use this 6-week action plan as a kick-start into your new lifestyle. It's simply a sort of preview that will help you iron out the kinks and work out the details so that you can stick to your guns. Even after the action plan is over, you must continue with this kind of a lifestyle and eat the type of foods prescribed here – only then can you maintain and sustain all the healing your body has undergone during these 6 weeks.

Another thing you must keep in mind is that every body is different. In the next couple of chapters we will see the major culprits in food substances that tend to trigger inflammatory responses – you should avoid them in general. However, identifying the exact trigger is something highly individualistic. You may not have a response to every added sugar, dairy product, gluten, etc. Once you complete your action plan, start slowly experimenting with foods to see which foods your body reacts to and then completely throw those out of your diet. If you wish to add the rest to your diet, you may, but *in moderation*. Once again, you don't want to slip back into your old habits and have inflammation flare up a second time!

Apart from food, the best way to keep your inflammation under control is by losing those excess pounds and regular exercise. For people with inflammatory tendencies, body fat can prove dangerous. Fats aren't always lethargic globules of flab. Trunk fat, especially, tends to be active tissue – it produces hormones and works actively, which means it can trigger inflammation, easily.

Working out regularly to get rid of those excess pounds will definitely bring down any inflammatory response you have! Also, keep in mind that maintaining a healthy weight will also lower your risk of cardiovascular diseases, which also triggers inflammation.

CHAPTER 2

FOODS THAT AGGRAVATE INFLAMMATION

There are certain types of foods that tend to trigger an inflammatory response within your system. Unfortunately, our day-to-day diets tend to be loaded with these. In this chapter, let's look at foods you must absolutely avoid during your 6 week meal-plan; go cold turkey with these foods! Once it's over, you can try slowly adding one after the other – in *small* quantities – to see which one is effecting your inflammation.

Saturated fats are a definite no. They increase your cholesterol levels and promote inflammation. Trans fats are equally worse; they send bad cholesterol soaring high and immediately trigger an inflammatory response within the body.

Omega-6 polysaturated fat is also another culprit. The problem is that most foods don't list Omega-6 specifically, instead just clumping them along with all polysaturated fats. Found in corn, sunflower, safflower and soybean oils, they litter the shelves of the grocery store and were, until recently, seen to be healthy fats. It's only now that we know that they don't help inflammation but instead boost it.

Sugar and simple carbs also make your inflammation spike. Refined sugar or foods with high glycemic index need to be avoided in order to help reduce the inflammatory response.

SPECIFIC FOODS TO AVOID

Below is a general list of things you need to avoid. To narrow it down further, here is a list of items that you'll want to avoid.

Red Meat contains high levels of Omeag-6 fatty acids that can cause severe inflammation. The quality of the meat is also important. Low quality meat can contain dangerous chemicals when processed, which can stimulate an inflammatory response.

Caffeine increases catecholamine, which is a stress hormone. This, in turn, elicits cortisol and brings up insulin levels, which automatically triggers inflammation. The acidity of coffee further worsens digestive discomfort, bringing problems such as heartburn. Even as little as one cup a day can trigger an inflammatory response. Switch to green tea instead – it has antioxidants that will help keep the inflammation at bay while still waking you the mornings!

Dairy is a huge inflammatory trigger for many people. Allergies to casein, gluten and the like are often the main reasons for inflammation. Lactose intolerance is another issue; keep away from all dairy products for 6 weeks and then see how much of a difference it makes!

Refined Grains are devoid of fiber and Vitamin B, unlike unrefined grains. In many ways, refined grain becomes similar to refined sugars – both have few nutrients and a high glycemic index. When you consume them regularly, they are bound to trigger an inflammatory response – avoid them.

CHAPTER 3

ANTI-INFLAMMATORY FOODS

In this chapter, let's take a look at the foods that are brilliant in fighting inflammation. Adding these to your diet is a must! Over the next 6 weeks, these are the foods you'll be adding to your recipes. Even after your 6-week period, make sure you eat these items regularly – they will keep the inflammation at bay and help you to remain healthy!

AVOCADO

Avocado contains five major nutrients – phytosterols, carotenoid antioxidants, non-carotenoid antioxidants, Omega-3 fatty acids and polyhydroxylated fatty alcohols. All five of these nutrients have been proven to fight inflammation in the body, especially when it comes to arthritis. Having one avocado a day can go a long way in helping you stave off your body's inflammatory response.

GINGER

Ginger contains gingerols, which are anti-inflammatory compounds. They are ultra-potent fighters and studies have shown that people who take ginger supplements on a daily basis see a marked reduction in their inflammation. They especially numb the pain from osteoarthritis and rheumatoid

, so add it to your staple consumption! Ginger can ly be used while cooking, especially in juices and smoothies, so don't turn your nose up at these snacks for lack of flavoring!

TURMERIC

Turmeric has powerful antioxidants as well as anti-tumor properties. It contains a pigment known as curcumin, which studies have proven to reduce pain and increase mobility, especially in people with osteoarthritis. Turmeric also blocks the inflammatory pathways and prevents the launch of the proteins that triggers the swelling and pain. It's antioxidant levels neutralize the free radicals, thereby bringing inflammation down. It's easy to add to your daily diet, so make sure your cooking includes it!

GARLIC

Garlic has anti-inflammatory properties that help in the prevention of obesity, protection of cardiovascular health, and reducing arthritis. Two compounds, vinyldithin and thiacremonone, inhibit the activity of the inflammatory messenger molecules – they block the pathways to swelling and their antioxidant properties keep the pain on a low scale. Allicin in garlic is the most infamous for its anti-inflammatory benefits, so make sure you add it to your daily flavors.

BEETROOT

Beetroot is also rich in antioxidants and contains the phytonutrients betanin, isobetanin and vulgaxanthin, which help with cardiovascular health. They also help in detoxification and have anti-fungal properties, so be sure to consume beetroot on a regular basis!

ASPARAGUS

Containing a variety of anti-inflammatory nutrients such as asparanin A, sarsasapogenin and protodioscin, asparagus has more than any other food in terms of protection! It also has a number of antioxidants such as Vitamins C, E and selenium, so it's an overall health food you cannot ignore.

FLAX SEEDS

Flax seeds are rich in omega-3 fatty acids and are some the best anti-inflammatory fighters around. The primary omega-3 in flax seeds is the alpha-linoleic acid – the ALA, which is beneficial for the cardiovascular system. It also helps in the prevention of excessive inflammation and protects blood vessels from inflammatory damage – so add flax seeds to your routine and make sure you consume them on a regular basis, also.

CINNAMON

Not only does cinnamon have antioxidant and antibacterial properties, it is also antifungal in nature and helps suppress appetite the natural way. It can help keep inflammation under control while also making sure you don't overeat or indulge!

GREEN TEA

Rich in antioxidants, green tea helps to lower cholesterol levels as well as prevent heart disease. It reduces inflammatory responses and has anti-cancer properties, which will keep you healthy for a long while. Switch from coffee to green tea, add a spice of ginger to it and you will find that it's just as effective as coffee for a kick of energy.

ORGANIC RED WINE

Surprise, surprise – red wine actually has antioxidants and anti-inflammatory properties! However, use it sparingly. One glass here and there will definitely help stave off inflammation, but too much and you'll feel the negative effects of alcohol ruining your hard work.

DARK CHOCOLATE

Cocoa, which is the main ingredient in dark chocolate, is extremely rich in antioxidants. It contains flavonoids called flavanols, which can help the cardiovascular system. Its anti-inflammatory properties, when you take it as an occasional indulgence, are something that is extremely beneficial – add a couple of nuts to it and you'll have an amazing snack that is both delicious and healthy!

CHAPTER 4

SIX WEEK ACTION PLAN

In this chapter, let's take a look at what your action plan consists of. You can try this plan for either a six or four-week period – it's entirely up to you. Remember, this interim period is only a jumpstart into a healthier lifestyle; going back to the junk you were eating isn't going to help with inflammation.

STEP 1 – RESTOCK KITCHEN AND GO GROCERY SHOPPING

We have discussed all those items that tend to trigger an inflammatory response in people. Sugars, transfats, omega-6, gluten, diary, etc., are all culprits that you need to throw out of your kitchen. Before you start healing your body via the food you're going to consume for the next few weeks, you'll need to remove any and all temptation from your pantry so that you don't fall back into the chasm of eating only junk!

Rid your kitchen of all the items we discussed previously. While it's possible that not all are actually causing your inflammation, at this point, it's better to go cold turkey for a while. After the 6 weeks are over, you can slowly start reintroducing them into your diet – in small quantities – to identify which items you're actually responding to. Once you've thrown out all the excess, make a list of items you need to buy for the next couple of weeks and go grocery shopping.

Here are a couple of things to keep in mind while shopping to help you follow through on your new diet:

- Always go shopping with a list. When you have a guideline in front of you, you're less tempted to veer away from it and won't end up adding those chips or mayo to your cart.

- Never, ever shop when you're hungry – at that point, everything looks good to eat! It leads to impulse buying, which you'll want to avoid.

- Even if it's just a weight loss diet that you're following and not an anti-inflammatory diet, it's a good idea to do your major shopping on the outer aisles of a grocery store where fresh fruits and veggies, lean meats, and whole grain breads are stored. The further into the grocery store you venture, you'll find the fattier and unhealthy foods.

STEP 2 – PRINT OUT BOTH MEAL PLAN AS WELL AS DAILY SCHEDULE

As I said previously, no diet can be undertaken in isolation. You need to be able to maintain the benefits you receive from this six-week period, so you'll need to make lifestyle changes to suit a healthier living. It's not just your diet you must modify – inflammation is also triggered by other factors such as lack of sleep, lack of exercise, etc.

The next step is to print out the daily schedule you'll be following and place it where you can see it regularly. The schedule itself is nothing special...

6.00 a.m. – Wake up and complete morning routines; exercise for a minimum of 30 minutes and breathe in as much fresh oxygen as possible.

7.30 a.m. – Breakfast

10.30 a.m. – Mid-morning Snack

12.30 p.m. – Lunch

3.30 p.m. – Mid-afternoon snack

5.30 p.m. – Quick evening workout (can be light)

6.30 p.m. – Dinner

9.00 p.m. – Late-night snack

10.30 p.m. – Bedtime

As you can see, it's very simple, following the age-old cliché of early to bed and early to rise. You'll need your daily 8 hours of sleep, no matter what. Exercise is important, too. If you've never worked out, you can start small by simply taking a walk around the neighborhood for 30 minutes. Don't expect too much too fast; that's the secret to any new diet regimen! The way you go about your day must be corrected just as much as your food patterns have to be corrected – only then will you be able to sustain the benefits you will reap from this diet!

Once you've printed out your schedule, take a look at your meal plan. At the start of every week, pick a set of recipes that you wish to follow for the week and tabulate it. We'll look at a lot of anti-inflammatory food recipes in the next chapter, but it's a good idea to plan out the entire week in advance. Not only will that help with grocery shopping, it'll also help ensure that you don't eat on impulse. Plan it out, print it and post it in a visible place in order to help you follow through.

STEP 3 – SAMPLE MEAL PLAN FOR A WEEK

Here's a sample of a meal plan that you can make for one week. The trick to sticking to a diet is to give yourself choices so that you don't feel like you're giving up anything. This is why we've listed a number of healthy and delicious recipes to choose from – pick and choose what you like and try out different combinations to keep things interesting!

Monday

BREAKFAST - Oatmeal with soy milk (top with ground flaxseeds, blueberry, banana, sprinkling of cinnamon; a cup of green tea

MID-MORNING SNACK - Handful of almonds

LUNCH - Spinach salad, with cherry tomatoes and grilled salmon; dress with virgin olive oil and lemon juice

MID-AFTERNOON SNACK - Green tea, with a pinch of fresh ginger, half an avocado on rye crackers seasoned with black pepper and red-chili flakes

DINNER - Chickpea and vegetable curry (use peas, spinach, sweet-potatoes, cauliflowers, etc.) with half-cup brown rice

LATE-NIGHT SNACK - Second half of avocado or a small glass of red wine

Tuesday

BREAKFAST - Poached omega-3 enriched organic eggs on tops of wholegrain bread; apple

MID-MORNING SNACK - Cup of green tea, hummus with carrot/cucumber sticks

LUNCH - Homemade Miso Soup (with soba noodles, peas, green onion, mushroom); salad topped with avocado, mango, cherry tomato, mixed greens, dressed with lime juice and olive oil

MID-AFTERNOON SNACK - Spiced watermelon with pistachio

DINNER - Wholegrain pasta (with kale, hemp, flaxseed oil pesto)

LATE-NIGHT SNACK - Cup of green tea

Wednesday

BREAKFAST - Smoothie with choice leafy greens, banana, seasoned with seeds like hemp/flaxseeds and cinnamon; a cup of green tea

MID-MORNING SNACK - Green tea; soy yogurt with blueberry

LUNCH - Leftover pesto pasta from previous day; pear/melon

MID-AFTERNOON SNACK - Hummus with sliced avocado/cherry tomatoes on rye crackers

DINNER - Steamed trout with ginger, chili, lime, soy sauce (serve with broccoli and sweet potato)

LATE-NIGHT SNACK - One square of dark chocolate (min 70% cocoa solids)

Thursday

BREAKFAST - Chia pudding made from soymilk, cinnamon and banana

MID-MORNING SNACK - Small apple and oat-bran muffin; cup of green tea

LUNCH - Vegetable and lentil soup; one orange

MID-AFTERNOON SNACK - Celery sticks, filled with almond butter

DINNER - Chicken fajitas with one chicken breast (organic), mixed veggies and spices, topped with salsa - serve in tortilla wraps

LATE-NIGHT SNACK - Cup of green tea

Friday

BREAKFAST - Raspberry and avocado smoothie; leftover pudding or soup

MID-MORNING SNACK - Cup of green tea; rice cake with almond butter

LUNCH - Chopped salad with baked tofu, almond-miso dressed - serve with wholegrain pita bread

MID-AFTERNOON SNACK - Spicy roast chickpeas; some berries

DINNER - Pan-seared fish, with shitake mushrooms - serve with sautéed green veggies/quinoa

LATE-NIGHT SNACK - Small glass of red wine

Saturday

BREAKFAST - Oats with soy milk or yogurt (top with nuts, shredded coconut, fresh fruit); cup of green tea with fresh ginger

MID-MORNING SNACK - Steamed edamame dressed with lime juice and olive oil

LUNCH - Lemon and herb sardine salad; one apple

MID-AFTERNOON SNACK - Tomato salsa with sliced bell peppers to dip

DINNER - Sweet potato, black beans and rice burger (wholegrain buns); sliced avocado and green salad

LATE-NIGHT SNACK - Cup of green tea

Sunday

BREAKFAST - Same oats with soy milk, top with nuts, berries, cinnamon; cup of green tea

MID-MORNING SNACK - One square of dark chocolate

LUNCH - Smoked salmon, dressed in greens and herbs, with lime juice and olive oil

MID-AFTERNOON SNACK - Handful of nuts

DINNER - Roasted red peppers, stuff with quinoa, cannellini beans; green salad with leafy veggies

LATE-NIGHT SNACK - Cup of green tea

Remember, this is just a sample meal. You can make your own meal plan with the recipes in the next section of the book!

CHAPTER 5

ANTI-INFLAMMATORY RECIPES

In this chapter, we'll take a look at the different types of foods you can make that are anti-inflammatory in nature. These are the foods you'll want to strictly eat over the course of the six weeks that you're on the diet. Once you've completed the six weeks, you can start experimenting and make your own recipes with the basic ingredients. Remember the foods you must strictly avoid; identify those that trigger an inflammatory response in your body; stay healthy and happy!

BREAKFAST FOODS

Cherry Coconut Porridge

Dried or fresh tart cherries contain anthocyanin, a powerful antioxidant known to cut down on inflammation.

Serves 4, with 300 calories per serving

Ingredients:

- 4 cups oats
- 4 tablespoons chia seed

- 4 cups coconut milk
- 4 tablespoons raw cacao
- Pinch of stevia
- Some coconut shavings
- Some dark chocolate shavings
- I cup cherries (either frozen or fresh)
- Maple syrup (for taste)

Instructions:

In a saucepan, throw in the coconut milk, chia seeds, oats, cacao and the stevia. Let it boil over a medium flame before bringing the heat down to a low simmer – keep this up until the oats are cooked. Once done, serve in a bowl, topped with the coconut/dark chocolate shavings, the cherries and the maple syrup to taste.

Raspberry and Avocado Smoothie

Avocado is one of the most powerful anti-inflammatory foods. Use unsweetened yogurt to bring down the sugar content. The drink will give you Vitamin C and fiber along with a hefty dose of antioxidants that will help fight inflammation.

Serves 2, with 130 calories per serving

Ingredients:

- 2 avocados (pitted and peeled)
- 1.5 cups orange juice
- 1.5 cups raspberry juice
- 1 cup raspberries
- 1 tablespoon cocoa powder (to taste)

Instructions:

Throw all the ingredients into the blender and blend until it becomes a smooth, creamy mixture. Add a tablespoon of cocoa powder to taste.

Gingerbread Oatmeal

Rich in Omega-3 fatty acids, this oatmeal is one of the best anti-inflammatory breakfasts you'll try.

Serves 2, with 150 calories per serving

Ingredients:

- 2 cups water
- ½ cup steel cut oats
- ¾ tablespoon cinnamon, ground
- 1/8 tablespoon coriander, ground
- 1 tablespoon cloves, ground
- 1/8 tablespoon ginger, ground
- 1/8 tablespoon allspice, ground
- 1/8 tablespoon nutmeg, ground
- 1/8 tablespoon cardamom, ground
- Maple syrup (to taste)

Instructions:

Make the oats as directed on the package; when it is boiling in water, add the spices. Once the oats are done, add a bit of maple syrup to taste.

Chia Pudding

Rich in Omega-3 fatty acids, this pudding is a great dessert as well as a light breakfast food you can enjoy, especially with all the fiber it adds to your diet!

Serves 2, with 206 calories per serving

Ingredients:

- ½ cup chia seeds
- 2 cups coconut milk
- 1 tablespoon honey
- ½ cup diced mango
- Handful of pepita seeds

Instructions:

In a small bowl, mix the coconut milk and the chia seeds and add a dash of honey to it. Leave it overnight in the fridge. In the morning, you'll find that the pudding has thickened and the chia seeds have gelled. Pour it out to serve and top with fresh mango and pepita seeds - you can top with any fruit and nut of your choice.

LUNCH FOODS

Mediterranean Tuna Salad

Tuna is an amazing source of Omega-3 fatty acids. This recipe is high in sodium so you can dial it down by choosing a low sodium canned tuna and also decreasing the quantity of capers and olives.

Serves 1 with 250 calories per serving

Ingredients:

- 1 5 ounce can tuna packed in water
- 1/8 cup chopped kalamata/mixed olives
- 1/8 cup mayonnaise
- 1 tablespoon red onion, minced
- 1 tablespoon fire roasted red peppers, chopped
- 1 tablespoon fresh basil, chopped
- 1 tablespoon capers
- 1 tablespoon lemon juice, fresh
- 1 large ripe tomato

Instructions:

Throw all the ingredients into a large bowl, except for the tomatoes. Stir nicely to combine; slice tomatoes into sixths, but don't cut all the way through. Gently pry them open and put the salad mixture into the center. Serve.

LUNCH FOODS

Mediterranean Tuna Salad

Tuna is an amazing source of Omega-3 fatty acids. This recipe is high in sodium so you can dial it down by choosing a low sodium canned tuna and also decreasing the quantity of capers and olives.

Serves 1 with 250 calories per serving

Ingredients:

- 1 5 ounce can tuna packed in water
- 1/8 cup chopped kalamata/mixed olives
- 1/8 cup mayonnaise
- 1 tablespoon red onion, minced
- 1 tablespoon fire roasted red peppers, chopped
- 1 tablespoon fresh basil, chopped
- 1 tablespoon capers
- 1 tablespoon lemon juice, fresh
- 1 large ripe tomato

Instructions:

Throw all the ingredients into a large bowl, except for the tomatoes. Stir nicely to combine; slice tomatoes into sixths, but don't cut all the way through. Gently pry them open and put the salad mixture into the center. Serve.

Kale Caesar Salad with Grilled Chicken Wrap

Kale is one of those leafy greens that is extremely rich in Omega-3. Use a gluten-free wrap to enjoy a quick and delicious meal!

Serves 1 with 200 calories per serving

Ingredients:

- 4 ounces grilled chicken, thinly sliced
- 3 cups curly kale, cut (bite-size pieces)
- ½ cup cherry tomatoes, sliced and quartered
- 1/3 cup Parmesan cheese, finely shredded
- ¼ coddled egg (cook for about 1 minute or so)
- ½ clove garlic, minced
- ¼ teaspoon Dijon mustard
- ½ teaspoon honey
- 1/8 cup lemon juice, fresh
- 1/8 cup olive oil
- 1 flat bread or 1 tortilla
- Salt and pepper (to taste)

Instructions:

    Mix the coddled egg, minced garlic, mustard, lemon juice, and olive oil and then add a drop of honey to the bowl. Whisk until a dressing has been formed and then season it with salt and pepper to taste. Now, add the kale, the cherry tomatoes and the chicken; toss it to coat with the dressing. Add the shredded Parmesan cheese and toss again to mix. Spread out the flatbread and evenly distribute the salad on top – sprinkle the Parmesan on top before rolling it and then slicing in half. Serve.

Winter Fruit Salad

Rich in antioxidants and low on c..., brilliant salad to take with you to work and toss together for lunch.

Serves 3 with 130 calories per serving

Ingredients:

- 1 cup persimmons, cut into 1 inch cubes
- 1 cup pears, cut into 1 inch cubes
- 1 cup grapes, cut into halves
- 1 cup pomegranate arils
- 1 cup pecans, cut into half and lengthwise slivers
- ½ tablespoon virgin olive oil
- ½ tablespoon peanut oil
- ½ tablespoon pomegranate-flavored vinegar
- 1 tablespoon agave nectar
- Pinch of salt, to taste

actions:

In a bowl, whisk the dressing ingredients – the olive and peanut oil, flavored vinegar and the agave nectar in order to blend the flavors. Cut the fruit and throw them into the bowl with the dressing and toss to mix. Toss in pecan pieces before you serve.

Roasted Red Pepper and Sweet Potato Soup

This soup, rich in antioxidants, can be frozen easily, so you can store it well in advance. Try using fresh roasted red peppers instead of from a jar in order to reduce the sodium content.

Serves 3 with 1200 calories per serving

Ingredients:

- 1 tablespoon olive oil
- 1 medium onion, chopped
- 6 ounces roasted red peppers, chopped
- 2 ounces green chilies, diced
- 1 teaspoon cumin, ground
- ½ teaspoon coriander, ground
- 2 cups sweet potatoes, peeled and cubed
- 2 cups vegetable broth
- 1 tablespoon fresh cilantro, minced
- ½ tablespoon lemon juice, fresh
- 2 ounces cheese, cubed
- Salt, to taste

Instructions:

Heat up the olive oil in a large soup pan over a medium flame. Sautee the onion until soft and add the red peppers, green chilies, coriander, cumin and salt to taste. Let it cook for about 2 minutes; stir in the reserved juice that is left from the roasted red peppers, broth and sweet potatoes. Bring the mixture to a boil; reduce flame to low simmer and cover, cooking for the next 10-15 minutes until the potatoes become tender. Pour the cilantro and lemon juice and stir; let it cool for a few minutes before pouring into a blender. Now add the cream cheese and blend until it turns smooth – pour back into the pot and heat for a few minutes. Season further with salt if required.

Whole Wheat Pasta with Super Kale, Hemp and Flaxseed Oil Pesto

Rich in Omega-3, protein, and good fats, this pasta will not only help reduce inflammation, but also help boost failing energy levels.

Serves 12 with 550 calories per serving

Ingredients:

- 6 cloves garlic, minced
- 6 cups packed kale
- 1½ cups hemp seeds
- 4 tablespoons lemon juice
- 1½ tablespoon fine-grain salt
- ½ tablespoon pepper, ground
- ½ cup flaxseed oil
- Red pepper flakes, to taste

Instructions:

In a food processor, add all the ingredients and then process until it reaches desired consistency. Next, cook the pasta according to its package instructions. Drain the pesto and add then mix together. You can keep the extra pesto in the fridge to be used later on sandwiches, wraps and salads.

DINNER FOODS

Curried Potatoes with Poached Eggs

Eggs have high Omega-3 content and you don't have to have them just for breakfast!

Serves 8 with 850 calories per serving

Ingredients:

- 4 russet potatoes
- 2 inches ginger, fresh
- 4 cloves garlic
- 2 tablespoons olive oil
- 2 tablespoons curry powder (hot or mild according to taste)
- 2 15-ounce cans of tomato sauce
- 8 large eggs
- 1 bunch cilantro, fresh

Instructions:

Wash and cut the potatoes in ¾ inch cubes and place them in a large pot filled with water. Cover the pot and heat until it boils; keep boiling until potatoes become tender. Drain the potatoes.

To make the sauce, peel the ginger's skin off and mince the garlic; add both to olive oil and sauté over medium low flame for about 2 minutes. Add the curry powder and sauté for another minute before throwing in the tomato sauce. Turn up the heat to a medium flame and let it cook for a minute or two before adding the cooked potatoes – if the mixture gets dry or too pasty, add a spoonful of water.

Next, make eight small dips in the potato mixture. Crack one egg into each of these and then cover the skillet, letting it come up to a simmer. Let it cook for the next 6-10 minutes. If you want a runny yolk, then remove earlier. Top the mixture with fresh cilantro and serve hot.

Baked Tilapia with Pecan Rosemary Topping

Tilapia has plenty of selenium, which helps improve arthritis symptoms. To avoid gluten, choose gluten-free bread.

Serves 8 with 210 calories per serving

Ingredients:

- 2/3 cup raw pecans, chopped
- 2/3 cup panko breadcrumbs
- 4 tablespoons fresh rosemary, chopped
- 1 tablespoon brown sugar
- ¼ tablespoon salt
- 2 pinches cayenne pepper
- 3 teaspoons olive oil
- 2 egg whites
- 8 4-ounce tilapia fillets

Instructions:

Preheat your oven to 350 degrees Fahrenheit. In a baking dish, mix the pecans, breadcrumbs and the brown sugar, seasoning with the salt and the cayenne pepper. Toss with olive oil and then bake the mixture until it turns a light, golden brown – it'll take about 7-8 minutes.

Bring the heat up to 400 degrees Fahrenheit and coat a large baking dish with cooking spray. Whisk the egg white in a shallow dish; dip the tilapia in the egg white, one fish at a time, and then dip again in the pecan mixture, coating each side equally. Now place this fish in the sprayed baking dish; press the remaining pecan mixture onto the top of the tilapia and bake it for about 10 minutes until it is cooked through.

Italian-Style Stuffed Red Peppers

Rich in protein and fiber, this is one dish that will boost your overall immunity.

Serves 12 with 150 calories per serving

Ingredients:

- 2 pounds lean ground turkey/beef
- 6 red bell peppers
- 4 cups Spaghetti sauce
- 2 tablespoons oregano seasoning
- 2 teaspoons garlic powder
- 1 cup frozen spinach, chopped
- 4 tablespoons Parmesan cheese, grated + 12 tablespoons to garnish each pepper
- Salt and pepper to taste

Instructions:

Preheat your oven to 450 degrees Fahrenheit. Line your baking sheet with foil and coat it with cooking spray. Cut peppers in half lengthwise and remove the seeds and ribs, setting them on the baking pan.

Cook the turkey/beef over a medium flame. Stir and break it up as it's cooking and when it's almost done, add the sauce and the seasoning. Stir till completely cooked and no longer pink in color – add the spinach and cheese and then stir until it's all mixed well.

Scoop up half a cup of this mixture and pour into one half pepper; sprinkle the rest of the cheese over it and then bake for 20-30 minutes, until the cheese melts and turns a light golden brown.

SNACKS

Whole Wheat Tortilla and Hummus

Hummus is ground chickpeas, which is extremely nutritious and helps boost immunity.

Serves 1 with 75 calories per serving

Ingredients:

- 1 whole wheat tortilla
- 1 cup hummus

Instructions:

Take one whole wheat tortilla and heat on skillet till it turns crispy. Break it up into pieces and spread the hummus on top.

Kale, Banana and Almond Milk Smoothie

Almond milk and fruit give you a healthy mix of fiber, protein, vitamins A, C and B, as well as Omega-3, which makes it a wonder drink!

Serves 1, with 150 calories per serving

Ingredients:

- 1 cup kale
- 1 banana
- 1 cup almond milk

Instructions:

Throw all the ingredients into the blender and blend until it becomes a smooth, creamy mixture.

Dark Chocolate and Nut Clusters

Dark chocolate, as we discussed earlier, is nutritious. It's a brilliant source of antioxidant, iron, magnesium and copper. And the nuts offer a variety of nutrients that make for a healthy and filling snack.

Serves 1, with 250 calories per serving

Ingredients:

- 1 ounce of dark chocolate
- ¼ cup almonds (or any nuts)

Instructions:

Melt your dark chocolate and pour into a bowl. Add the almonds and mix together. You could go for a set of mixed nuts or pick any nut of your choice.

Spicy Watermelon and Pistachios

This nut and fruit combination, with added cayenne pepper, is not only tasty, but also boosts immunity and is extremely nutritious!

Serves 1, with 75 calories per serving

Ingredients:

- 1 watermelon
- 1 tablespoon lime juice
- 1/2 tablespoon grated lime zest
- 1 teaspoon cayenne pepper
- 2 teaspoons roasted pistachios

Instructions:

Cut the watermelon up into little chunks and add a single tablespoon of lime juice. Throw in half a teaspoon of the grated lime zest and 2 teaspoons of roasted and unsalted pistachios. Season with cayenne pepper and enjoy!

CHAPTER 6

THINGS TO REMEMBER DURING YOUR SIX WEEK ACTION PLAN

It's easy to say that you're going to go on a six week action plan that will kick start a new way of life for you. But it's much harder to actually to stick to your guns. Remember, the idea is to use these six weeks as a precursor to a newer, healthier lifestyle, so you cannot slip back into older diets and habits when the six weeks come to an end. Here are a few things that can help...

ESTABLISH A SUPPORT SYSTEM BEFORE YOU BEGIN

Obviously, you cannot go to it alone. Sometimes, we all need that extra push to make sure we follow through on our goals – establishing a good support system during these six weeks will definitely help! Rope in a friend or a family member who will be willing to work with you. It could be something as simple as encouraging you when you are having cravings or having friends actually join you on the six week diet; a diet partner. When you are running low on willpower, your peers and family can pick up the pieces and help you out!

EXPERIMENT WITH THE RECIPES

The biggest problem people have with diets is the fact that they find them too restrictive. We have already seen how you can modify a number of recipes to include anti-inflammatory foods. We have listed a number of foods that are rich in anti-inflammatory properties. You can look up additional foods and then play with them to make your own recipes and make fun dishes that are delicious. As long as you feel like you're not making a big sacrifice by not eating your regular junk and you find that you have alternatives to offer your palate, you definitely won't give up on your diet!

MAINTAIN A FOOD JOURNAL

This is an excellent way of tracking your inflammatory patterns. When you write down your cravings, as well as what you are actually eating, you'll learn what your addictions are and how you can avoid them. Keep logging in these details even after your six-week action plan is over. A journal will be especially important once you start introducing the foods you had eliminated; your body will react. Maintaining a food journal will help you identify which items cause the worst symptoms and which items you can eat on moderate basis. This way, you can come up with a long-term anti-inflammatory food plan that will keep you healthy and fit!

CONCLUSION

Inflammation is a sneaky thing to fight – you'll have to work hard to identify your triggers and avoid them completely. For the six weeks that you will be on an anti-inflammatory diet, things are going to be relatively easy. Once you complete your diet, that's when the challenge begins – you'll need to start thinking long-term food plans to make sure you don't slide back into your old aches and pains!

Eat healthy, sleep well and make sure you exercise daily. These are the staples for avoiding inflammation. Use the recipes given in this book to keep your inflammation under control. As you slowly master the art of healthy cooking, you can experiment and make your delicious dishes as suited to your particular palate!

I wish you best in your new adventure!

Finally, if you enjoyed this book, then I'd like to ask you for a favor, would you be kind enough to leave a review for this book on Amazon? It'd be greatly appreciated!

Click here to leave a review for this book on Amazon!

Thank you and good luck!

PREVIEW OF "TEA CLEANSE"

TEA CLEANSE

7 DAY TEA CLEANSE DIET: HOW TO CHOOSE YOUR DETOX TEAS, BOOST YOUR METABOLISM, LOSE 10 POUNDS A WEEK AND FLUSH OUT TOXINS

INTRODUCTION

This book contains proven steps and strategies on how to choose your own Detox regimen to boost your metabolism, lose ten pounds as well as flush out the toxins in your body.

There are different ways to jumpstart and speed up your weight loss. Have you ever heard of natural fat and calorie burners? No other book can share with you the real secret towards losing the bloat and burning the fat to make sure the weight does not come back.

The artificial way of losing 10 pounds include drinking slimming pills, going to the gym almost every day or starving yourself. Are you tired of trying out any fad diet that comes your way? If you have answered yes, now is payback time. Included in this book are tea cleanse recipes that guarantee the desired weight loss.

This will be a diet program that must be strictly followed to achieve an impressive 10 pound weight loss. Just imagine the different recipes that were designed to be low on the taste part but high in the brand-new you. This program is designed for you to eat food that tastes good while at the same time, does some serious cleansing to your body. It is low in calories yet allows you to feel full.

Be ready to adjust your pants a couple of inches smaller. Several tea recipes and healthy smoothies are provided in this book to make your mornings worth waking up to. They taste so good you will actually forget that you are on a diet. What are you waiting for? Start the 7 Day Tea Cleanse. To weight loss and good skin, this is for you!

Check out the rest of Tea Cleanse on Amazon.

CHECK OUT MY OTHER BOOKS

Below you'll find some of my other popular books that are popular on Amazon and Kindle as well

Tea Cleanse: 7 Day Tea Cleanse Diet: How to Choose Your Detox Teas, Boost Your Metabolism, Lose 10 Pounds a Week and Flush Out Toxins

Whole: 30 Day Whole Food Diet: Whole Foods Cookbook for Beginners, Tasty Recipes to Lose Weight Eating Whole Foods

Diabetes: Step by Step Diabetes Diet to Reverse Diabetes, Lower Your Blood Sugar and Live Well

Bone Broth: Bone Broth Diet Cookbook: Bone Broth Recipes and Guide to Lose Up 15 Pounds, Firm up Your Skin, Reverse Grey Hair and Improve Health in 21 Days

Atkins Diet: Atkins Diet Weight Loss Plan with Delicious Recipes to Permanently Change Yourself

Mediterranean Diet: Recipes and Diet Guide for Weight Loss and Healthy Eating

Ketogenic Diet: Ketogenic Weight Loss Diet, Avoid Mistakes & Live Healthier

Vegan: Vegan Diet Cookbook for Delicious and Healthy Recipes

Made in the USA
San Bernardino, CA
14 December 2016